COLORADO

Scenic Wonderland

COLORADO

Scenic Wonderland

Featuring DAVID MUENCH Photography

Text by Paul M. Lewis

Published by Beautiful West Publishing Company
2994 Lennox Road, Eugene, Oregon 97404
Robert D. Shangle, Publisher
ISBN 0-915796-07-4 (Soft Cover)
ISBN 0-915796-08-2 (Hard Cover)

DAVID MUENCH

David Muench received his early training from his father, the distinguished photographer of nature, Josef Muench. For several years young David accompanied the elder Muench on trips through the West, receiving thereby an incomparable education in landscape photography.

His enduring love for nature gained on these early excursions is reflected in his photography, regularly published in magazines like ARIZONA HIGHWAYS, NATIONAL WILDLIFE, and AUDUBON. David's work has also appeared in books, calendars, and other publications.

The pictures in this book have been selected from his extensive library of western landscape photographs.

CONTENTS

CREDITS

Photography by David Muench
Color Separations by Pacific Color Plate, Portland, Oregon
Lithography by Durham and Downey, Portland, Oregon

COVER: Sunrise ignites a blaze of yellow on the rolling floor of Dallas Divide as low-hanging clouds brush the crest
of the Sneffels Range in southwestern Colorado.

INTRODUCTION

Colorado's natural endowments are so varied that the task of organizing them into a short descriptive framework is overwhelming. The state has more diversity in its makeup than almost any comparable land area on the continent. The famous high, dry climate, with its moderate temperatures, makes Colorado a delightfully comfortable place to live. But there are some spots that are very cold, and some that are very hot. Elevations go from 3,350 to past 14,000, from prairies to foothills to Mountains (with a capital M). Heavy precipitation is restricted to mountainous regions, and rainfall ranges widely from miniscule (7 inches annually in the San Luis Valley) to generous (27 inches annually at Silverton, in the San Juans).

The superlative settings come in many shapes, materials, and colors. Deep canyons, high mountains, broad valleys, mesas, and prairies are all represented. The rocks of the Rockies are of many varieties: limestones, marbles, granites, lavas, and sandstones. And a kind of mineral wealth never dreamed of by the first, frantic gold and silver prospectors is being extracted: lead, zinc, copper, coal, petroleum, and natural gas, in addition to some of the minerals essential to today's exotic technologies — uranium, vanadium, and molybdenum. So far, more than 3,000 species of flora have been identified in Colorado's five plant zones, from the plains to the alpine reaches. And both mountain and plains areas support diverse animal communities.

So Colorado, with its variety of natural gifts, has been attracting many sorts of inhabitants for a long time. When the last glaciers retreated, 10,000 or so years ago, the region became the home of several Indian cultures comprising plains, desert, and mountain tribes. Before the coming of the white man, the Cheyenne, Arapaho, Comanche, and Kiowa moved into the plains and plateaus, along with (to a lesser extent), Pawnee and Sioux. The Utes, the only tribe indigenous to Colorado, ruled the mountain areas. Though the Indian inhabitants probably never numbered much more than 10,000, their tribal groupings represented different traditions and life styles, from the nomadic societies who depended chiefly on hunting to the farming tribes of the mesaland who built permanent dwellings and practiced irrigated agriculture.

When man came in force, he represented even greater cultural disparity. The first great invasion — the ore hunters — was aptly characterized by Horace Greeley during the Colorado segment of his trip across the country in 1859. Greeley sounds astonished as he writes in his journal of the various seekers after gold:

> Ex-editors, ex-printers, ex-clerks, ex-steamboat men . . . omnibus drivers from Broadway . . . ex-border ruffians from civilized Kansas. All of these, blended with veteran mountain men, Indians of all grades from the tamest to the wildest, half-breeds, French trappers and *voyageurs* . . . and an occasional Negro, compose a medley such as hardly another region can parallel.*

*Horace Greeley, *An Overland Journey*, ed. Charles T. Duncan, New York, 1964, p. 132.

Men and women of different origins and viewpoints have continued to be drawn to Colorado from that day to this. Perhaps Colorado's heterogeneous citizenry of today have contributed to the unusually mature outlook of a state that has paused amid the rush of modern life to take stock. Greed, opportunism, and the pressures of civilization have inflicted scars on Colorado as they have on many of our beautiful natural treasure-houses. But, the short- and long-term population and energy demands of continued growth have lately created a powerful corps of dissenters within the state. Environmental issues are being opposed to the thesis that development is all. This was dramatically illustrated by the rejection, in a 1972 statewide referendum, of the 1976 Winter Olympic Games.

The wilderness grandeur of Colorado is unique. The developing sense of stewardship in Colorado and elsewhere is helping to safeguard that fragile beauty. This book might serve as a reminder of what is at stake. Here, photographer David Muench offers his very personal interpretations of some of Colorado's landscapes. It is hoped that these beautiful and exciting compositions will record, not a setting that is disappearing, but one that will be there for many ages to come.

Opposite:
Nymph Lake in Rocky Mountain National Park shows off its flotilla of water lilies. Just behind the lakeside hills, Hallette Peak juts starkly into the sky like an elemental spirit of the mountains.

Pages 10 & 11
A brash lunar orb appears to be competing with the late afternoon sun by an untimely moonrise over the snow-clad San Juans in Dallas Divide. Yellow-tinted cottonwoods and reddish-brown foothills suggest the changing season.

Page 12   (Upper) Miners' shacks and other weathered buildings pose wearily as relics of the past in Tincup, Colorado, a town located in the Sawatch Range.
(Lower) A sea of yellow rabbitbrush flows around the base of the proud Sierra Blanca like so many worshippers before a majestic white goddess. The immense, sharp-edged mountain, in the Sangre de Cristo Range, has its winter robe of snow, as does the valley floor.

Page 13   A sparkling little alpine brook drops over a series of mossy banks in Yankee Boy Basin of the San Juan Range.

Page 14

Snow-laden evergreen boughs frame a part of Cliff Palace in Mesa Verde National Park. The stone apartments were built by prehistoric Indians who lived and farmed in the Mesa Verde area.

Page 15

(Upper) Snow-mantled Chair Mountain (13,500 feet) provides a backdrop for the brilliant cotton-wood foliage along Crystal River near Redstone. This autumn scene was taken in White River National Forest. (Lower) Round cactus in springtime flower provides a dazzling red highlight to the varied green tones of the San Juan country in south-western Colorado. The Sneffels Range rises across the valley.

Pages 16 & 17

A long line of aspens with their golden yellow foliage stand at attention in this autumn tableau taken at Snowmass Canyon near the Aspen ski area.

Page 18   (Upper) The silt-laden Green River winds along its spectacular canyon in Dinosaur National Monument. At this point, below Harper's Corner, the Green has been joined by the Yampa River and is on its way west into the Utah portion of the Monument.
(Lower) The vivid blue of Trapper Lake and the emerald green of its forested shore provide a delicate contrast to the elemental, bare rock of the White River Flattops.

Page 19   Colorado's famed Maroon Belles tower like a rocky chorus line above Maroon Creek and Lake in the White River National Forest of the Sawatch Range. Snow emphasizes the layered profiles of these peaks, all over 14,000 feet.

ge 20
head frame raises its
eleton against the sky
ove Leadville, a center
Colorado's silver mining
activity. The burned
d weathered stumps in
e foreground are remind-
rs of forest devastation
at occurred in the area
ring mining operations.

ge 21
pper) Golden brown
tumn pastures spread
t under a sky of broken
uds in the South Park
ea of the Rockies.
ower) The brilliant
ndstone hues of Gateway
cks are a striking
ntrast to Pike's Peak,
the near background
e red rock structure is
Garden of the Gods, a
ouping of tilted rock
rmations that were
rmed when the Front
nge was being created.

ges 22 & 23
nrise etches the colorful
ffs and monoliths of
onument Canyon in
lorado National Monu-
ent. Independence
ck is in the center.

SCENIC SPECTACULARS

Rocky Mountain National Park, the most extensive of the wilderness areas in Colorado, is 405 square miles of mountains, lakes, forests, chasms, meadows, and streams. It takes in an area enfolded between the Park and Front ranges in north-central Colorado. The national park is a sanctuary for a variety of wildlife, including bear, deer, bobcat, mountain lion, bighorn sheep, and elk. The town of Estes Park is a main eastern entrance to the area. As with many such jumping-off places, Estes Park is jammed with tourists (80,000) every summer day. Many of the travelers never get any farther than this very commercial and touristy town, whose 4,000 inhabitants extract enough loot from the travelers to keep themselves in plenty of provisions for the winter.

The highest continuous highway in the country winds through Rocky Mountain National Park. This is Trail Ridge Road (U.S. 34), following a serpentine, up-and-down course, offering startling vistas of the Continental Divide, and passing Grand Lake, one of the highest lakes in the world. From points on the highway one may penetrate the wilderness on foot and merge with timeless nature. Or the visitor may stay in his car and drink in the majestic scenery, watching 1,000-foot chasms drop away from the road as it winds along over the tundra at 12,000 feet (at times), near the windy ridge lines, in a treeless, alpine setting. In summer, masses of tiny wildflowers provide an additional visual feast. Some of the high-country residents are sometimes seen — marmots, the rabbit-like pikas, and ptarmigans.

A spectacular and intimate river canyon environment is present in the far northwest corner of Colorado. Dinosaur National Monument is a conglomerate of weird and dazzling rock structures and breathtaking vertical canyons. The Monument is an ideal meeting ground for man and nature in close proximity. Some of the other mighty river canyons of the West display themselves in arrogant and diffident splendor, where the visitor can only stand off and admire. At Dinosaur, explorers may either hike the rim or explore the bottom of the canyon walls; or they may ride down the white water of the Green and Yampa rivers, the two wild streams whose flashing waters have cut the amazing hanging canyons and rock cliffs along their courses. Dinosaur is somewhat misnamed, having originally been designated a monument in order to protect the fossil dinosaur bones discovered there. The preserve was later enlarged to include all the Green and Yampa river canyons.

Near Grand Junction, midway along the western border, the Colorado National Monument displays its own version of canyons, escarpments, and giant pillars of sandstone. A rimrock drive affords sweeping views of the Monument's natural wonders and encourages imaginary journeys in time back to the age of the dinosaurs.

Page 24   An old barn and weathered fence railings blend into this gentle pastoral scene on an autumn morning in the San Miguel range. The shining spire in the distance is Wilson Peak.

One of Colorado's gorges of particularly stunning visual impact is the Black Canyon of the Gunnison National Monument, near Montrose in the southwest. The canyon is aptly named. The gorge is so narrow that it is lighted only briefly by the noonday sun, when the red, pink, and gray veins of its granite walls are revealed. At other times it is lost in deep shadow. The canyon's awesome beauty stretches along ten miles of the Gunnison River. It can be studied from rim drives or by trail, looking down at the river 2,000 feet below. The trail, along the edge of the north rim, leads to the point where the gorge is only 1,300 feet across. Some of the bravest (or most foolhardy) visitors to the canyon are known to creep down the nearly vertical wall to investigate the dark floor and the river itself. The Gunnison is a tributary of the Colorado, joining that powerful waterway, appropriately enough, at Grand Junction.

The southwest corner of Colorado contains Mesa Verde National Park, 80 square miles of both aesthetic and historical pleasure. The park country includes table land and hilly, wooded areas, with juniper forests and sandstone. It is renowned for its remarkable cliff dwellings known as Balcony House, Cliff Palace, Spruce Tree House, and Square Tower House. These apartment houses in stone were occupied by the Basket Weavers and later the Pueblo Indians of the Anasazi culture. The Anasazi ("Ancient Ones") were corn and bean growers, having abandoned their nomadic hunting life earlier. They lived in this and in other areas of west and northwest Colorado for some 1,300 years. They vanished rather suddenly, possibly moving on after a series of drought years in the latter part of the 13th century, and raids by hostile tribes of Navajos and Apaches.

Sand dunes are accepted phenomena of the world's seashore and desert regions. At first acquaintance the proper conditions would not seem to be present in an area like Colorado to make their formation likely. Yet an area of 57 square miles in the San Luis Valley contains the largest dune formations in the United States. This is the Great Sand Dunes National Monument, just under the western slope of the Sangre de Cristo Range. The dryness of the valley floor has fostered a sandy situation, and prevailing southwest winds have picked up the sand and dropped it at the base of the mountains. The resulting dunes keep on growing, some now as high as 600 feet. When the wind blows through the dunes at night, whistling and whining up against the jagged mountains, the natives tell eerie tales to travelers, of ghostly herds of sheep, and horses with webbed feet, haunting the sands during the darkest hours.

We tend to think of scenic beauty as an extravaganza of vast perspectives that bowls over the observer with the sheer power of its presence. That is undeniably one aspect of beauty. Another kind of natural charm comes in smaller forms. And in Colorado these forms make a large contribution to the lavish portions of enchantment that capture the eye wherever one ventures in this phenomenally gifted state. The breathtaking mountain uprushes, the stomach-dropping depths of river canyons, the powerful streams, and vast prairie lands owe part of their charisma to the tiny plants that grow on mountain slopes, on canyon walls, along the banks of waterways, and in waving masses on the endless plains.

Wildflowers. All over Colorado they appear in myriad forms and colors. With five plant zones, Colorado has more than its share of floral beauty. To catalog them is unthinkable in this small space, even if the writer were capable of it. For example, some 500 kinds of plant life grow on the prairies. The cactus comes in 24 varieties in Colorado. Some of the springflowers are the sand lily; the evening primrose, in cream or rose pink; the coral-colored wild geranium; buttercups, and the white star flower. The hotter-weather species, like the sunflower, the purple-tassled scotch thistle, devil's claw, and loco weed, bloom up to midsummer. In the most arid plains areas grow the cocklebur, silvery sage, mesquite shrub, bush morning glory, and the talented yucca plant, put to so many uses by the Indians.

Some of the profusion of dazzlers that dress up the lower slopes are Indian paint brush, mountain rue, woods violets, foxglove, blue bells, wild roses, Mariposa lilies, brown-eyed Susan, and mountain daisy. In the high valleys and along streams are found lady slipper, calypso, and lady's tresses. In summer, the high mountain meadows are covered in lavish yellow with the alpine gold-flower. Also among those present are the purple anemone, the white marsh marigold, the yellow monkey flower, and the alpine primrose.

Individually these small residents of the plains, forests, or mountain meadows are shy and retiring, but being sociable, they usually prefer to live with many others of their kind. Their gracious presence helps build the mystery and awe the wilderness explorer feels when he enters the domain that owes nothing to man.

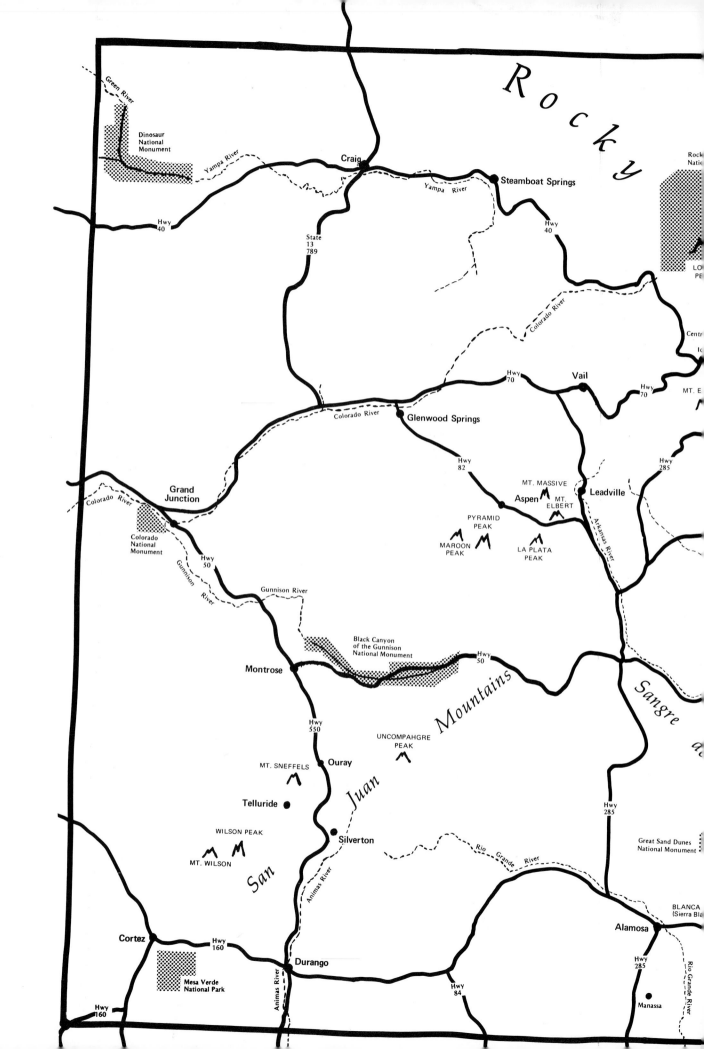

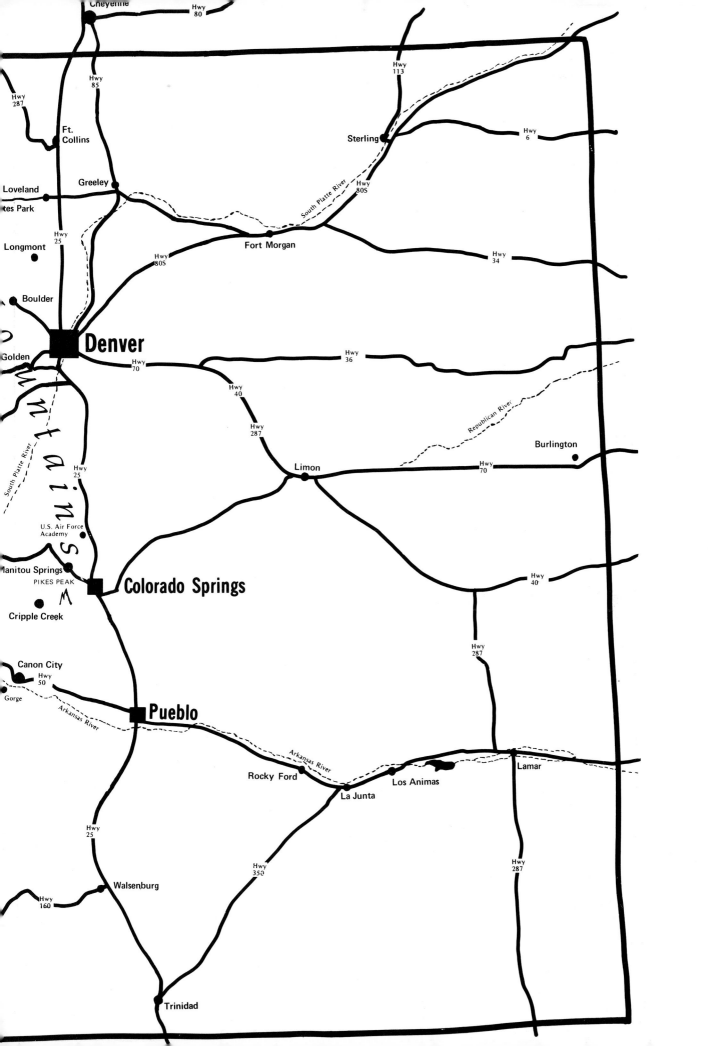

DENVER, AND COMPANY

The hump of the Rockies divides Colorado into halves. East of the barrier stretch the Colorado plains; to the west, more mountains, broad valleys, mesas, and spectacular river canyons. The "Shining Mountains" of the Indians dominate all of this, determining the weather and well-being of all they survey. Along the north-south wall of the Front Range, have grown most of the biggest towns. Backed against the eastern flank of the mountains, these cities line up on the edge of the plain partaking of both environments. Here live the majority of Coloradans — in Ft. Collins, Greeley, Longmont, and Boulder in the North; Denver and Colorado Springs in the center; Pueblo and Trinidad in the south.

Denver is the capital of Colorado and Queen City of the Plains. Its population is more than 500,000, about a fourth of Colorado's two million human inhabitants. Camped within hailing distance of the Front Range, it sprawls on an oasis of the high plains watered by Cherry Creek, flowing northwestward, and the South Platte River, heading to the northeast. In this mile-high oasis, at the confluence of the two streams, Denver had been used as a meeting place long before the white man became interested in it. Denverites are fond of the notion fostered by some accounts that the town was founded "on a jumped claim." The record does show that a group of sharks from Kansas territory, headed by William H. Larimer of Leavenworth, simply confiscated claims previously staked out on the north and south banks of the two streams by speculators with future gold strikes in mind.

If Denver got off to a shaky start, you wouldn't know it from the city's proud place in the glittering ranks of America's notable towns. Manufacturing, mostly of the highly specialized kind, is the activity from which Denver derives much of its income. Since World War II, the highly technical aerospace industry has been centered here, along with military installations and industries producing sophisticated military material. And many federal agencies have their headquarters here, so that Denver is becoming known as a "second Washington." As a result, Denver has more scientists and specialists — by percentage at least — than any other American city. The superlative educational institutions in the area — Denver University, the Colorado School of Mines, and the nearby University of Colorado at Boulder — contribute a great deal toward the high rate of literacy and sophistication.

One of Denver's legitimate boasts has to do with climate. Colorado is an inland state, with no water of any significance outside of the supply stored in the mountains. So Denver is high and dry. Even if it sometimes gets very hot or very cold and snowy for short spells, the dryness of the air makes things comfortable. But to most people who live in this clean and bustling city, the basic environmental attraction is, always, the Mountains. Denverites are mountain-lovers, even if some of them don't necessarily go physically into the Rockies any oftener than the average Manhattanite heads up into New Hampshire's White Mountains. The Rockies are simply there, a monumental and beautiful backdrop to the city, awesome and inviting all at once. And that's enough for some city-dwellers who have yet to take their first hike into the Front Range. A great many Denver people do join their brethren from the "Springs," Pueblo, and other east-slope towns for vacations in the Rockies, where they act like people do in most of the scenic places of the West, taking the well-trodden pathways into the organized playgrounds on the fringes of the wilderness. There they boast to the out-of-staters of the incomparable beauties of Colorado while grumbling about how the overcrowding is spoiling "their" mountains.

Like other free-swinging western towns, Denver has a colorful past. Unfortunately, that fiendish necessity of modern living, the auto, has dictated the shape of the city's profile to a great extent, leaving fewer and fewer buildings around that stand as witness to that past. Among the relics that have disappeared are the Tabor Opera House, built by the flamboyant "Silver King," the Mining Exchange Building, and the Windsor Hotel, all making way for parking space. But Denver's cultural and historical concerns are well represented by outstanding museums and galleries. Among these are the Denver Museum of Natural History, the Colorado State Historical Museum, and the Denver Art Museum, all in the company of the finest institutions of their kind.

Colorado Springs, some 55 miles due south of Denver, is the champion attraction for tourists — Coloradans and others — in the state. More accurately, the town and the nearby Air Force Academy taken together exert this pull on sightseers. Known to Coloradans simply as the "Springs," this beautiful community is noted for its fine climate, winter and summer. It is a starting point for trips to Pike's Peak, Garden of the Gods, and Cripple Creek, (all mentioned elsewhere), and for mountain drives that add to appreciation of the area's scenic riches. The Will Rogers Shrine of the Sun and the Seven Falls of Cheyenne Canyon are also nearby.

Pueblo, 42 miles south of the "Springs" on the main north-south highway, doesn't have the scenic splendor of its neighbor. Pueblo is a working town, situated in flat, arid country. A railroad and steelmaking center, it supplies many of the things that Coloradans and people around the country need. The smoke and soot of Pueblo cause a kind of negative pride in the various kinds of pollution Pueblans encounter in their city. With all that gorgeous scenery, clean air, and snowy mountains around every place else, cosmopolitan Pueblo is "different."

Clustered to the north, between Denver and the border, are the two big college towns of Boulder and Ft. Collins, plus Greeley and Longmont. Perhaps even more well known than any of these is a smaller town between Longmont and Ft. Collins named Loveland. Loveland has, of course, a very special postmark — a branding iron with an L in a heart — that gets a lot of extra use around Valentine's Day when romantic messages are remailed here from all over the country. The civic fathers of the "Sweetheart Town of the Nation" support these image-creating activities carried on by the residents. There is some irony in that name — its original possessor was a steely-tough railroad robber baron.

Colorado is, more than any other state, a skiing center. The Colorado Rockies are dotted with ski slopes, and many of these areas have been developed, especially in the west-central regions of the state. Two mountain towns, Vail and Aspen, have emerged as skiing capitals of the world. Both areas are gaining stature as year-round resorts, with a variety of summer activities. At Vail, for example, there are the usual summer pursuits suitable for the mountain outdoors, like fly fishing, hunting, and back packing. Golf and tennis are offered, too — not your usual high-altitude sports. Aspen for many years has drawn summer visitors interested in its cultural activities, including offerings in the humanities and musical studies and events. The Aspen Music School attracts students from this country and abroad.

Lordly Mt. Abrams dominates this Uncompahgre River Valley setting where the gold mining town of Ouray is dwarfed by the powerful sweep of the surrounding mountains. Winter has designed this snowy scene in the southwestern Colorado Rockies.

Page 34   (Upper) Autumn and winter fight for attention here. Massed yellow foliage covers a slope below the snow-streaked
                 faces of the spectacular Maroon Belles in Colorado's Elk Range.
                 (Lower) Spectral shapes seem to swirl over the valley floor as the sunrise touches the sand sculptures of Great Sand
                 Dunes National Monument. The Sangre de Cristos wait in the background for the day to break over their rugged faces.
Page 35   The Green River rushes along the bottom of the Gate of Lodore in Dinosaur National Monument.
Pages 36 & 37   Mt. Hayden in the San Juans sits for an autumn sunrise portrait.

Page 38
(Upper) The peaks of the Sneffels Range, gleaming with a fresh coat of snow contrast vividly with the green carpet of quaking aspen on the rolling hills around them. This view is along State Highway 145 near Telluride.
(Lower) The headwaters of the Arkansas River flow out of a bleak winterscape on their way to the east and eventual juncture with the Mississippi. The big, long Arkansas rises near Leadville directly out of the Continental Divide. Mt. Elbert, monarch of the Rockies at 14,431 feet, provides the back-drop.

Page 39
Bridal Veil Falls drops straight down 365 feet at Pandora Basin near Telluride in southwestern Colorado.

Pages 40 & 41
Crystal-clear Molas Lake reproduces the sharp points of the Grenadiers in its calm waters, with its own green bank and lakeside evergreens thrown in for good measure. These peaks are part of the San Juan Mountains.

Page 42   (Upper) Autumn sprinkles the state capitol grounds in Denver with golden leaves.
                    (Lower) The famed mining community of Telluride nestles in the lee of Ajax Peak (12,785 feet) and Telluride Peak (13,200 feet). The town is located in the San Miguel River canyon.

Page 43   The Sneffels Range in southwestern Colorado is the setting for this glimpse of broken autumn sunlight.

Page 44   Sheep graze on spring pastureland near Telluride. The far background reveals snowy Bald Mountain.

Page 45   Harper's Corner in Dinosaur National Monument is a dramatic example of the maze of canyons cut by the Yampa and Green rivers in their meandering courses.

Page 46
(Upper) Pawnee Butte
rides like a battleship over
the brown sea of Pawnee
National Grasslands, and
flotillas of storm clouds
build up over the mountain
in the summer skies.
(Lower) A spring pastoral
setting lies nestled under
the sheltering wall of foothills and mountain peaks
in the Uncompahgre River
valley. The Sneffels Range
clad in white, provides a
wintry touch offsetting
the gentler mood of the
rest of this scene.

Page 47
In Vail, travel is simplified
up the slopes by tram car,
down by ski. This world-
famous resort vies with
Aspen and other mountain
areas of Colorado for the
multitudes of skiers who
are making their sport one
of the state's major industries.

Upper   Clusters of anemone and rydbergia hold up their bright
             faces along Cottonwood Pass of the Sawatch Range.
Lower   Showy red Indian paintbrush turns an aspen grove into
             an enchanted forest at Rabbit Ears Pass.

Upper   Cow parsnips stand out against aspen boles in the
             San Juan Mountains.
Lower   The harsh profiles of the Maroon Belles are softened
             by a carpet of anemone in the alpine meadows of the
             Maroon-Snowmass Wilderness.

PICTURESQUE PEOPLE
AND PLACES

I t's a truism that man, especially western man, can and does alter his environment to suit his desires and needs. Things could possibly be the other way around in Colorado. The white man's civilization that made its way into the territory brought with it an amazing assortment of individuals whose lives were changed by this rugged land's vast possibilities.

Whether this bit of folk wisdom in reverse is worth considering for longer than a millisecond, one fact is undeniable. Quite a few of the figures who have peopled the so-called civilized history of Colorado make a good case for the way this up-and-down region shapes personalities. The process, of course, is still going on. Colorful characters are not limited to a certain era of the past, but today's worthies have yet to receive the definitive outlines wrought by a certain distance in time.

The lure of gold and silver, at its zenith in the 1850s, was the single most important catalyst in bringing the white man's civilization to the territory, although the beaver trappers, or mountain men, blazed the trail in the Rockies earlier in the century. Today the town of Central City stands as a monument to the first great gold-inspired (and misdirected) stampede into Colorado — the "Pike's Peak or Bust" rush of 1859. The mining community, a few miles west of Denver, grew up around the first big gold strike in Colorado. This discovery, in what came to be known as Gregory's Gulch, turned out to be a gold mine, so to speak, for one John H. Gregory. Gregory's dogged determination, persistence, and hard work finally made him wealthy. From his vein of lode gold and others established in the Gulch, about 85 million dollars in ore was extracted. Gregory was a hard-bitten mountain man who worked alone. He resented the "trespassers" who swarmed into the Gulch after his find was reported; he resented others reaping the fruits of his patient, difficult search. But his resentment stopped short of the dollar, and he made a fortune by selling rights to his original mine and to others in the area. "Green" Russell, a gold prospector from Georgia who had traveled over much of the Rockies with his party looking for the precious metal, established a claim in a nearby area, later named Russell Gulch. His find was even richer than Gregory's original one. Russell, a cosmopolitan, educated man in marked contrast to Gregory, was just as rugged and determined. His interests extended beyond the hunt for gold. His land speculations in this area involved him in the founding of the nearby community of Auraria, "twin" of Denver City.

Two well-known journalists, Horace Greeley and Henry Villard, helped swell the rush to the gold fields. Their reports, though cautious, fostered the legend about the bonanza lying there for the taking in Colorado Territory. Faulty geography apparently was responsible for steering many of the thousands of neophyte prospectors to the

Pike's Peak area to the south. The celebrated slogan, "Pike's Peak or Bust," turned out to be ironically prophetic for those unfortunates who headed in that direction.

The first person to flash the story of Gregory's gold was William N. Byers in his *Rocky Mountain News*. He beat the opposition to the streets in Denver with the news on May 28, 1859. Byers is one of the big names in Colorado affairs of this period. His newspaper, now one of the West's most distinguished, promoted Denver City and the Territory as desirable places for settlement. He used the gold fever to further this idea, taking visiting newspapermen like Henry Villard in charge when they came to inspect the Gregory Gulch operation.

Central City still is in business today, but a different business. It is now a successful tourist attraction, along with the nearby town of Blackhawk. During the season, the two "ghost towns" draw many thousands of visitors to the mountain environs where 15,000 persons once lived. Victorian homes of the original residents are in evidence, hanging onto the steep hillsides. The Central City Opera House is further evidence of the town's free-spending origins. It is used today for operas in which artists from New York's Metropolitan perform, and for hit plays from Broadway. The Teller House, built in 1872, and a very posh place in its time, still fulfills its original mission as a bar and hotel. The famous *Face on the Barroom Floor* was painted there by artist Herndon Davis in 1936 as a prank.

Central City is another one of Colorado's altitudinous towns; its elevation is 8,500 feet. Abandoned mining sites such as those at Russell Gulch can be visited via an unpaved road from the town. As would be expected, the scenery is on the awesome side in this vicinity, and motorists who travel the short distance to Idaho Springs are well rewarded for having to maneuver down a road full of hairpin curves. The fall season is the best time for visual delights, when the hillsides are golden with aspen leaves.

One of the first great entrepreneurs of Colorado's mining days arrived in 1859, in time to take advantage of the discovery of extensive silver veins. H. A. W. Tabor, the "Silver King," born in Vermont, came to the area stony-broke, but was soon tremendously wealthy as the result of grubstaking silver prospectors. His name is connected primarily with Leadville, the nearly two-mile-high (10,200 ft.) silver town southwest of Denver where he operated his own mines and sold supplies to silver miners. Leadville, nicknamed "Cloud City," became the center of mining as gold veins gave out and attention shifted to silver. Tabor's original investment was less than one hundred dollars' worth of food and tools, for which he acquired a third interest in a multimillion-dollar producer.

Of the mines he sank himself the most famous and probably the wealthiest (monthly yield, $100,000) was the Matchless. After Tabor acquired a fortune he shed his wife, Augusta, married his mistress, Baby Doe, built an opulent opera house in Leadville, a more opulent one in Denver (in 1881), and bought himself an appointment as an interim United States senator (Colorado became a state in 1876). His diversified financial interests eventually included real estate, insurance, and banking. His ostentatious mode of life was a far cry from Vermont. He left an example of conspicuous consumption that self-made millionaires in and out of Colorado have been trying to live up to ever since. He died broke, by the way.

The mining communities were surprisingly placid. Though there were prostitution and plenty of liquor and saloons, many of the miners brought their families as soon as they could, and lived sober lives, in every sense of the word. In some places, much of the mining population was of Scottish and German descent, and apparently had the single-minded devotion to a goal supposedly characteristic of those national groups.

One exception to this, in the silver era, was the town of Creede (in the San Juan Range), founded in 1890 in southwest Colorado and named after Nicholas C. Creede, who discovered the "Holy Moses" vein of silver there in 1889. Creede became well known for violence and prostitution, with an army of prostitutes headed by a tall, thin woman called "Slanting Annie" — she walked bent forward.

The Holy Moses mine was thus named when Creede used this biblical expression upon finding his silver lode. Many of the mines, gold and silver, bore such names of emotional impact. Earlier on, for example, the "Eureka!" mine (an exclamation point seems called for) had brought forth that outburst from one Henry Gunnell when he panned his first gold. Gunnell's instincts were good — he became wealthy from his vein. There must have been quite a few mines dubbed "Gawdamighty," "Holy Cow," "Ferhevvinsake," and "Geewhiz" in those feverish days.

In the early 1890s, when the silver boom started to go bust, because of various economic factors, the last and richest gold mining district — Cripple Creek — was born. The town, west of Colorado Springs, is now a tourist attraction with its abandoned mines, tailings, and preserved examples of the buildings of that era. In its heyday Cripple Creek and its sister towns had 20,000 inhabitants. In 1895 its mines yielded six million dollars, seven million the next year, and about 15 million dollars a year for the next decade. To date, some 300 million dollars in gold has been dug out of the hillsides here. Once close to ghost-town status, Cripple Creek has become a thriving tourist stop. It is still remembered as it used to be by a few people who were there. Mabel Barbee Lee's books, *Cripple Creek Days* and *Back in Cripple Creek*, are highly entertaining remembrances of the period. Mrs. Lee was encouraged in her writing by Lowell Thomas, who was born in Victor, a nearby town in the district. Among her vignettes is one of Jack Dempsey, who hails from the tiny town of Manassa in south-central Colorado, close to the New Mexico border. The Manassa Mauler recalls some highlights of his early career as a professional boxer in Victor.

The San Juan Mountains, in the southwest, yielded some of the richest gold and silver lodes of the last century. Mining operations are still going on at some sites. This is the case at Camp Bird Mine, near the mile-and-a-half-high town of Ouray, one of the important mining centers. Camp Bird is where Evelyn Walsh McLean's father, Thomas Walsh, made his fortune. At its peak period, the mine produced four million dollars a year in gold.

Ouray itself is noteworthy for more than its mining past. It is in the heart of the magnificent "Switzerland of the Rockies." (see pictures, pages 33, 63) Within a short radius of the town are scores of peaks, some more than 14,000 feet high. Ghosts of southwest Colorado's silver mining bonanza can be found on the slopes and in the valleys near Ouray. Ruined buildings bear witness to former towns, and headframes mark old mines.

In the San Juan basin, near the Ute Indian Reservation, is the former wild-and-wooly frontier town of Durango, now a trading and tourist center. Durango is the starting point for a memorable 45-mile train trip to the Silverton, another celebrated mining town. The narrow-gauge Rio Grande line snakes along the steep canyon of the Rio de las Animas Perdidas (River of Lost Souls), now called simply the Animas River. During the summer, a train of antique coaches, pulled by a chugging steam engine or two, puffs up the canyon to Silverton daily, crowded with railroad buffs and tourists. This is one of the few remaining branches of the rail lines that were built to carry ore during the silver boom of the 1870s. The excursion train returns to Durango in the afternoon, after the passengers have had a chance to visit in Silverton, looking into souvenir shops and abandoned buildings, visiting the museum in the Grand Imperial Hotel, and otherwise getting the feel of one of the legendary mining communities.

MOUNTAINS, MOUNTAINS

Major mountain groupings that dominate the Colorado landscape are not so much ranges as great, irregular ridges interspersed with high valleys or "parks." Their separation in space and differences in the matter of formation, however, allow distinctive labels to be given them. The Front, Park, and Sawatch ranges are closely grouped in a north-south direction. They enclose a long, high valley that extends north into Wyoming and south to the Sangre de Cristo Mountains. This intermontane area is divided into three distinct basins called parks — North, Middle, and South. They contain the headwaters of major rivers: the Platte in North Park, the Colorado in Middle Park, and the South Platte in South Park. These high meadowlands have relatively stable temperatures and moderate precipitation, protected as they are by mountain peaks around them. A fourth such "park" is the San Luis Valley, between the Sangre de Cristo Range and the San Juan mountains.

The other two major ranges in Colorado are the Sangre de Cristo, continuing the Rockies' eastern face to the south; and the San Juans, a mountain group in the southwest.

For most Coloradans, the most familiar mountains are in the Front Range, simply because it is closest to the biggest towns and therefore more accessible than the other Colorado Rockies. Its high wall stretches from the Laramie Range in Wyoming to the Colorado Springs area. Along its extent are hundreds of great peaks around 14,000 feet or better, the most lofty being Longs Peak (14,256 ft.). Longs Peak is one of the select number of spires that offer climbers a serious challenge — its precipitous east face, the Diamond, is straight up and down for 1,700 feet. More widely known than Longs, but no climber's mountain, is majestic Pike's Peak, rising from the plains at the southern end of the range. It's a mere 14,110 feet, but its separation from other mountain ridges gives it a commanding appearance. The peak is named after an army lieutenant with the musical name of Zebulon Montgomery Pike, who is credited with its "discovery" (although the Spaniards said they saw it first, if you don't count the Indian tribes who were around before anyone else). Zebulon Pike was exploring the Louisiana Purchase in 1806 for the United States government. Traveling up the Arkansas River he eventually reached the mountain that was to bear his name. The lieutenant said at the time that the mountain was unscalable. Now the fattest and laziest tourist can get to the top without even an extra wheeze or puff. During the season, an automobile can be driven up the mighty mountain, or one may take a nine-mile trip to the summit in a cogwheel train.

The celebrated peak overlooks another "spectacular" near Colorado Springs — the Garden of the Gods. Here, beautiful red sandstone formations are canted skyward, somewhat like "flatirons," pushed up by the same pressures that raised the whole Front Range. Another distinctive grouping of these structures, up north near Boulder, is named, with admirable descriptive insight, "The Flatirons."

The Sawatch and Park ranges form the long western wall of the high valley between them and the Front Range. The Sawatch includes the highest point of the Rockies, Mt. Elbert (14,431 ft.) and is associated with many of the extensive gold and silver discoveries in 1860 and 1877. Nearly as high, and nearby, is Mt. Massive (14,421 ft.), silver ore repository and backdrop for the mining town of Leadville.

Two rugged and remote mountain groupings dominate the south-central and southwestern regions of the state. The Sangre de Cristo Range flows down into New Mexico and forms the southern terminus of the Rockies. Its name ("Blood of Christ") is believed to derive from early Spanish explorers, awed by the dazzling effect of the late afternoon sun on its peaks of deep-red rock. The colors are emphasized by the sharpness of the crest and fold lines of these mountains. The peaks are precipitous, rising with dramatic sweep from the valleys around them.

The San Juan mountains occupy much of the southwest, across the broad San Luis Valley from the Sangre de Cristo Range. They are much more irregular in form than the other ranges and represent many different groupings, among them the La Plata, San Miguel, Needles, and Sneffels formations. The San Juans are considered by many Coloradans as the most spectacular mountains in the state. This is also a favorite recreational area. Within a few miles of Durango, southwestern Colorado's big town, the high wilderness beckons with the lure of fishing, hunting, skiing, and exploring.

THE OTHER SIDE

East of the Rockies, immense stretches are given over to the high Colorado plains. Part of the swath of high and dry plains that cut through the middle of the United States, they form a different Colorado from the one that tourists flock to and wilderness explorers search out. Horace Greeley was one of those 19th-Century travelers who were impressed with the harsh face of this "American Desert." In 1859, when he took his own advice and went west, the renowned newspaperman wrote in his journal after arriving in eastern Colorado (then Kansas Territory):

> We left this morning, Station 17 . . . at least thirty miles back, and did not see a tree and but one bunch of low shrubs in a dry watercourse throughout our dreary morning ride, till we came in sight of the Republican (River), which has a little — a very little — scrubby cottonwood nested in and along its bluffs just here . . . Of grass there is little, and that little of miserable quality — either a scanty furze or coarse alkaline sort of rush, less fit for food than Physic.*

Horace and many others before and since who have come upon this part of the continent thought of it as another Sahara. This was a bit unfair. Those easterners who, like Greeley, were used to defining landscapes at least partially in terms of trees, had some difficulty in relating to a land without them.

In our day this trackless terrain is a little less so because of man and his works. But it still imparts a feeling of endless space and solitude. As for the desolation that Greeley remarked upon, it is only apparent. Many stretches of the plains yield up crops: alfalfa, wheat, corn, hay. Man has brought water to some areas, from the Rockies or by tapping underground sources, to force the soil to cooperate. The high Colorado plains were built up many millions of years ago partially by deposition from the waters of the Rockies. Another part of the buildup is attributed to glacial loess left behind by the retreating ice mass and blown hundreds of miles over the area.

The human population of the Plains is thin. One may drive for many miles over flat or gently rolling stretches without seeing another car, another person, or even a house. Human habitation is signaled by the roadside telephone poles and by occasional cultivated fields dotting the open prairie. In the north, east of the town of Sterling, this is the look of things. The area has most of the dry farming potential of the eastern regions. Here the dry farmer takes careful advantage of the low annual rainfall and of underground water, adopting farm practices that conserve moisture.

The lower valley of the South Platte runs across the northern Colorado Plains. Its rolling hills and lowlands support lush farms whose fields are irrigated by water from the river. This valley grows more sugar beets than most other areas of the country, drawing migrant workers of varied ethnic backgrounds from Colorado's cosmopolitan population. Some of them — Slavs and Scandinavians — live in the "sugar towns" of this region; others, like the Spanish-Americans, move up for the season from the southern parts of the Colorado. Growing sugar beets formerly required a great deal of

*Horace Greeley, op.cit., p. 81.

Page 55

hand labor. Now the uprooting and topping is done by tractor-drawn machines. The beets are processed in several towns along the river, including Sterling, the biggest (about 12,000).

Outside of the irrigated belt of the river valley, northeastern Colorado is not hospitable to farming. Much of the area's prairie grassland was destroyed by would-be homesteaders of the last century who tried to cultivate it. Water was too much of a problem, and by breaking up the protective grass matting of the surface the cultivators exposed the soil to high winds. Erosion increased year by year and dust storms became regular occurrences.

The central regions of eastern Colorado are, if anything, even more arid. More open prairie is the case. But even in this part of the state, what was once part of the "Great American Desert" is encouraged, here and there, to grow crops like wheat and corn; some oats, rye, beans, and barley are also raised on the dry farms. Farther south, along the route now known as U.S. 40, the dry, open land took on a particularly grim aspect to the hordes trekking west to the Colorado gold fields in the 1850s and 1860s. Especially during the ill-fated Pike's Peak Gold Rush of 1859, many ill-equipped and inexperienced fortune-hunters died of hunger and thirst trying to cross this part of Colorado. Some, too, were killed by Indians enraged by the invasion of their buffalo hunting grounds.

The southern region of the Plains, once the scene of enormous cattle grazing operations, are now given over mostly to agriculture. The valley of the Arkansas River dominates this area, supporting irrigated farms, dairies, and lamb and poultry raising. In Rocky Ford, for example, the primary business is the growing of vegetables and flowers for seed.

The extreme southern part of eastern Colorado is in the former "Dust Bowl." Though the terrifying dust storms of the early 1930s no longer make their visitations in force, they are not yet a thing of the past. The fragile topsoil of the Plains here, as farther north, was torn away by man's ill-conceived farming ventures. The area is slowly recovering, partly because of increased rainfall in the past few decades. The whirling dust, when it does come, is no longer the disaster it once was. The "desert farmers" of Colorado have reclaimed much of the land, and the Dust Bowl drought is apparently over.

Page 57   Brilliant reds and golds create an autumn explosion of color along Red Mountain pass in the San Juans. Red Mountain, at top of the picture, raises its snowy dome over Ironton Valley.

Pages 58 & 59   Looking like scoops of vanilla fudge ice cream, the Maroon Belles double their dazzling symmetry in the glacial waters of Maroon Lake in the West Elk Range.

Page 60
(Upper) The Rio Grande
River rushes across a high
valley of southwestern
Colorado, near the silver
mining town of Creede.
Mountains of the San Jua
group rise around the
stream.
(Lower) Unique shapes a
brilliant colors are featur
of Garden of the Gods, n
Colorado Springs. The re
sandstone forms of Gate
Rocks find a counterpois
in the grayish-white silt-
stone structure nearby.

Page 61
Winter's frosting sets off
Trout Lake and its retin
of mountain peaks in the
San Juan Range of south
western Colorado.

Page 62   The weathered relic of a head frame stands defiantly amid the evergreen grandeur of Mineral Creek Canyon in southwestern
            Colorado's San Juan Mountains.
Page 63   (Upper) Ouray, a community celebrated in Colorado mining history, seems to be part of a Swiss landscape in this view
            showing the steep slopes of the San Juan Mountains enfolding the town in their protective embrace.
            (Lower) A sudden storm has left a coating of snow on the rolling plains of the Dallas Divide and on the Sneffels Range.
Pages 64 & 65   Cliff Palace, the best known of Mesa Verde's cliff dwellings, is brought to life again by a brilliant summer sun. These
            amazing cliffside apartments were constructed by the Anasazi Indians, a farming culture of the Pueblo Indians.

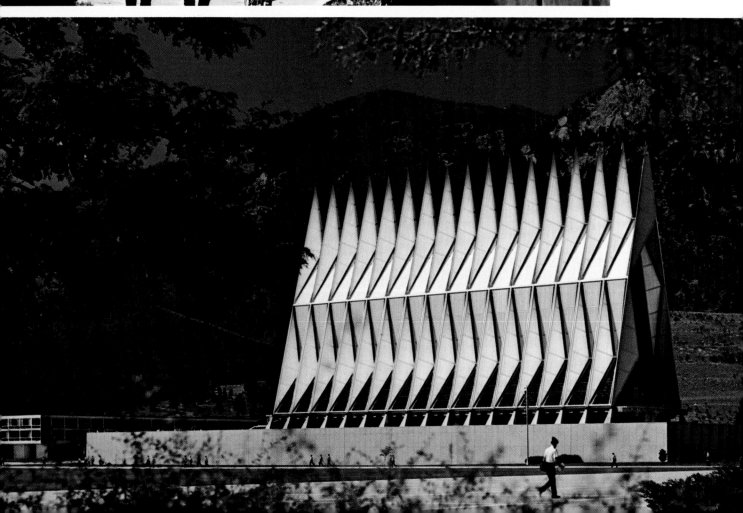

Page 70   (Upper) A gentle autumn sun warms a soft, pastoral tableau of grazing cattle against rolling uplands dressed in dense yellow foliage. The scene is Crystal River Canyon (Chair Mountain).

(Lower) Pyramid Peak and the Maroon Belles are seen from Buckskin Pass in the Maroon-Snowmass Wilderness.

Page 71   The waters of Chasm Falls turn to foam as they leap the cataract of Fall River in Rocky Mountain National Park.

Page 72   A rolling, tree-covered valley, part of the forested highlands of Rocky Mountain National Park, is glimpsed through a rock cut in the surrounding mountain wall. Mt. Ida and Mt. Julien form the crest across the valley.